tongue &
groove

T0097904

also by Stephen Cramer:

Shiva's Drum (2003)

tongue & groove

| poems |
by

Stephen Cramer

University of Illinois Press
Urbana and Chicago

Library of Congress Cataloging-in-Publication Data
Cramer, Stephen, 1975–
Tongue & groove : poems / by Stephen Cramer.
p.   cm.
ISBN-13 978-0-252-03236-3 (cloth : alk. paper) —
ISBN-10 0-252-03236-5 (cloth : alk. paper)
ISBN-13 978-0-252-07473-8 (pbk. : alk. paper)
ISBN-10 0-252-07473-4 (pbk. : alk. paper)
I. Title. II. Title: Tongue and groove.
PS3603.R365T66   2007
811'.6—dc22   2007016983

acknowledgments

Many thanks to the editors of the following journals in which these poems first appeared, sometimes in earlier versions:

Artful Dodge:	"Cloisters" "East River View: Renditions"
Asheville Poetry Review:	"Ascension"
Atlanta Review:	"*The Mustard Seed Garden Manual of Painting*"
Barrow Street:	"The Painters at MoMA"
Green Mountains Review:	"Wheels"
Hayden's Ferry Review:	"Glass of Milk" "Imprint"
High Plains Literary Review:	"Missing It"
The Literary Review:	"Glaciers"
Mid-American Review:	"Satin"
North American Review:	"Kneading"
South Dakota Review:	"Getting Over"
Southwest Review:	"Mockingbird"

"Before You" appeared in *Blues for Bill*,
Kurt Brown, Meg Kearney, Donna Reis, Estha Weiner, editors,
Akron University Press 2005.

| for joey & the whales |

tongue & groove

noun A type of construction consisting of two pieces,
one with a convex "tongue" and another with
a concave "groove" which, when joined, fit securely
and durably, creating one continuous whole.

tongue

verb (slang) To kiss passionately.

groove

verb (slang) To move with a pronounced rhythm,
usually in concert with music.

contents

I

II

III

Seams of Departure

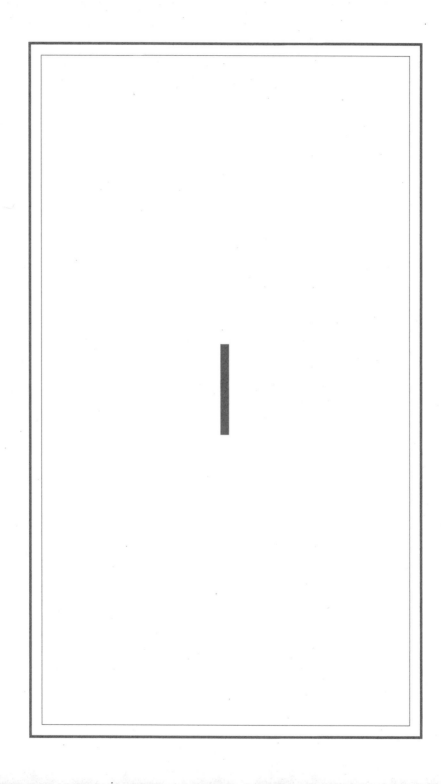

Wheels

The doors labor open to the heaped
        clamor of commute—conductor's
    drawl & static, the PA leaking

crackled locales &, below that, more urgently,

      a metallic rasp & chafe—kneeling there,
        a man on a make-shift contraption
    (plywood base, shopping cart wheels) pulls off
the painstaking work of carting himself

across the gapped threshold. Swaddled
        in a blanket—someone's beat-up
    woolen blue—he wheels his bulk

on fisted knuckles to the pole's brief

      mooring. That's when the blanket
        falls & what's left of his legs
    pokes through like stout elbows.
By then there's no need

for pageantry, but when he reaches
        the car's middle (there's no one,
    now, who isn't watching) he begins,

gently as his weather-worn voice will allow,

      to sing. Nothing intricate or too
        creative, this unadorned loop
    of a song's just enough to contain
the four recurring lyrics—*I got*

no legs. He lifts his eyebrows
                  like a choirboy, distinctly
            proud, before repeating

the simple fact of it—*I got no*

            legs. And as he sings, he rows himself
                  forward like the song's scant exhalation,
            & not his blackened fingers,
propelled him. Imagine the intricate

travelogue of those wheels—
                  stippled asphalt, cobble, curb
            & impossible staircase—the endless

caterwaul of friction a sort of kindred

            music to him. Slick linoleum rumble
                  as he threads through the aisle,
            clutches the handle, hazards
the gap to the car in front.

We don't even need to watch
                  to see how the blanket drops,
            the exertion of retrieval, the routine

culminating in four unreeled syllables

            that let you forget any touch
                  of affectation. Because, showbiz
            aside, he's answered fate not
with complaint or lamentation,

ʹbut with song (& let's not pretend—oh yes,
   it's coming: there's something out there
  with our names on it): & we all

need a song that says *mercy.* Song

  that says *O veiled & fathomless*
   city, strangely bejeweled by such
  sundered & dazzling creatures,
hear our simple pleas because

there's a legless man in the next
   car & I can't stop feeling
  how our bodies speed

through the space his just held,

  how he's the part of us
   that's gotten there first.

Getting Over

Overcharged bass fizzles to static—
    someone's scowling boombox
(oversized accessory) blares
    across the Ave., hammered

    & flagrant, pure adrenaline
doled out to three-minute doses.
    It's torch, rave & grind,

& somehow the raucous beat
    lends structure to lower Manhattan's
uniquely hip breed of ruin, shattered
    brick abloom with graffiti's sprawled

    roster. One wall's a rollcall
of encrypted initials—letters entangled,
    conjoined in a mesh

of stealth & sweat.
    They call it *getting over*
in the protean vernacular
    the street serves up,

    compendium of verbal strut.
It's as primal as the bass's
    continuous detonation, the urge

to make your fixed
    mark—even prehistoric craftsmen
crushed glowing cinders with berries,
    mixed myth & embers

till cavern walls thundered
with hooved glyphs. For what? Luck
    in the hunt, to outlive the body's

disrepair, to allure a woman
    &, come on, tell the truth,
have we added anything more
    to our tally of ambitions?—

    because, Honey, that hurt's
going down all over
    these streets, the East Village

& its 10,000 ways to say
    check me out—magenta hair cresting
in frosted peaks, sad indigo
    & blur of inked skin,

    the endless configurations
of the verb *I am*. What's graffiti
    but a sort of amplified

makeover, a front to extend
    beyond that passing
shield of skin? I don't care
    who you are, we're all getting over

    something in this town, & this wall's
disheveled peak (rouge syllables
    spoken again and again

from brick) only proves it.
    Someone here—a friend
grasping his ankles—hung inverted
    to vertigo's blood rush & panic

    & listen: if that's what it takes
to join this millennium old tribe,
      to go on in this city

of wreck & fever,
      then go seek out
what scares you most
      & spray, chalk, paint yourself in.

    Don't think twice or
look both ways.
      Just weave with your fist

that crucial name,
      immortal
on those crazed
      & train-shook windows.

Glaciers

Purely glacial, this basin
        & ridge—you & I tramping
   among scraped testimony

of the ice's halt & retreat,
        the channel carved for run-off
   so the stream can keep breaking

& healing itself over a stone.
        A butterfly catches an updraft,
   all swivel & glint, one of dozens

in this ravine returned from Ontario.
        Imagine their mass-migration—
   Lake Superior, the orange swarms

methodically dogleg
        on an invisible hinge—shrewd
   clouds, their hindbrains

still harbor blueprints
        of a glacier long gone.
   I can't grasp that ice's

ancient haul, but I can feel
        our lives' steady pull.
   We're in deep

woods now—antler, scat & bone—
        papers somehow conferring
   this feral stomping ground

to our name, & you're as good
               as gliding among rhododendron
       & fern, tracing all that isn't there:

wall & foundation. Brief gust
               & the leaves are a gold & russet
       dervish skewed & reskewed. But

before we begin, you must know:
               I'm awkward with a hammer
       & my right angles slope

even with a T-square, the level's lime-
               green bubbles forever misaligned.
       Love, only now I'm learning

the ways of lasting construction:
               dovetail, double tongue & groove,
       & you don't need a hammer

to build what we're building.
               What steers us, unseen
       but solid as bedrock?

Let's make our move
               now. In my chest I can feel
       a billion trembling wings

veering at once.

Mockingbird

You keep it up
you gonna get your ass
broke some huffing Mama
warns & grabs her pre-
teen boy by the back
of his head so he hurries
back to her side
like he got the wrong
end of a wishbone
when all he's doing
is nosing his way through
a street-side table
where a man's hawking
jasmine & patchouli
lifting vials & chanting along
with the static thump
of an over-sized boom box
but who needs all
the buzz of tinctured
desire these days when even
the puffed-up mockingbird
on the fire escape's cascade
unreels his chain-linked
repertoire with some avian
version of tough-guy swagger
because this year when
there's hardly been a breath
between thaw & burgeon
you're as good

as dead if you can't feel
spring barreling
13 miles a day
straight into your gut
& I want to tell the boy
that some people
walk around dead
in this pulsing burning world
but you never
have to recover
from astonishment
never
so go ahead & dedicate
your version of this ghetto-blaster's
song to the salvation
of your mother's swing
because you got to
take in what you hear
& belt out as your own
a version that's been forged
in your muscles
& brewed in your blood
& Mama let me tell you
that ain't no joke
& *ain't no ass*
gonna get broke

Satin

I hope he makes it through,
whoever on a dare
spray-painted on the school,
shamelessly as one ever could,
the word "satin."
Between an anarchy sign
& a crooked swastika,
this is no devil,
but just might be the meanest
glossy fabric in town.

What hope do you have
when you're wrong
at your most passionate?
Sweet screw-up, I send you
all the hope in the world.

Strings

The ukulele's got no strings,
so this skewed version of a recital
should be severely unmemorable:

a man in the museum kneeling
before the Tibetan Wheel of Life,
cradling his instrument,

carving a gradual arc into the wood
as his thumb & index finger
strum the barren gap

to a continuous chafe & grind.
Curious music as the sullen
ruins of his cracked face

search the mural—the chalk & glue
buffed to glaze, the coral spokes,
the hub reeling in ash: curious

music as figures plummet on one side,
are broken beneath the rim
then rise, buoyant, on the other.

Maybe that's why he's here:
to ensure in the next crank
of that great wheel—that brief

cleft of no breath & the dizzy
rebirth—he'll buoy toward
a sturdier frame.
                    On the stairs out front,

a throng of folks I'll never get to be:
hip tongue-stud lisp & delinquent
stare, those on the curb

waiting for some form
of transport that keeps on
not arriving, all these people

lashed to the whirl
of this city, repeat & repeat
to the shattering, & how broken

do we need to get
before we roll out of the depths
& rise, because on these streets

don't even *think* about looking
for a next life—Sweetheart,
you ain't gonna get it—

& all you can do is prepare
to be astonished out of your body
& into another's, to feel your way

into something as remote
as the grayed & toiling flesh
still grinding away at that scored

& barren wood—phantom
strings & phantom resonance.
& if you can give

that pent-up music outlet
& so completely enter
into that other life,

if you can recover those lost chords
his hands could never express,
then who's to say you can't

ride that wheel
straight to liberation: song
that goes from his sliced

fingers into the wheel's
root-ground ambers, song
that goes from his shortening

breath straight to my voice,
song that seems to endure
with us a while then leave us

but this man feels—now I feel—
it can never really leave,
song that just goes, baby,

it just goes & goes & goes.

The Mustard Seed Garden Manual of Painting

Entangled hemp fibers. Ax cuts. Horse

teeth. In this 17th
           century Chinese guide,
brushstroke labels almost outpaint

the works themselves.

           Small eddies
it prescribes for apricot foliage or,
for the ridged gleam

           of a trout's fanned tail,

liquid rivulets. Engaging, these descriptions,
but they're hemmed in
           by such a slew

of intricate instructions

that the pupils' works are bound
           to be interchangeable.
Where, then, the departure,

the discovery of contours

           unknown, where the path
into your own, made
wilderness of ink?

           In the Asian garden,

manicured to the last spore of moss,
a fountain churns
                    the central pool

stocked with minnows—minute tiers

of silver shimmer,
                    striated & tapered, none,
even in their gilt prismatics,

distinguishable

                    from the rest. & how
is their repeated flesh any different
from the rash facsimiles

                    this brushwork requires?

This manual expounds an art
not of innovation
                    but of expanding

awareness. Know, that means, the caterpillars

that spun the silk
                    you paint on, the mulberry
on which they fed. Know what herbs

gave their only roots

                    to be ground
into this very ink. (Such spells of attention
meant to wrench you

                    from your frame

so you enter, for a few astonished
breaths, the scene
                    you're bent to capture.)

The pool's fish, at the merest shadow's

approach, veer at once
                    in a single multi-finned
feint, one reflex extended between

a dozen bodies.

                    Not a single one
could (or would ever want to) stand out.
& maybe—so foreign

                    to our cult of self-

gratification, our endless *I me mine*—
maybe *that's* the manual's
                    aim—to set aside,

for a moment, innovation & wear instead

grand namelessness.
                    Are you prepared,
a slick of bruised peach tipping

your brush, to be astounded

                    out of your skin?
Enough of this same old
making new.

                    Let these copper fins

lavish a familiar current, tread the same
ancient cascade
            that plunges & spills,

as it must, & can never run dry.

The Painters at MoMA

We view their work the most,
though it never inspires
the dazzle of camera flash

like the hyperbolic wheeling,
the furious burn & swirl

of that famously heaving
night sky. Their work is never
complete, & I'm not talking

rumors of unsatisfied masters
entering the galleries

with a crimson-lit brush
stashed beneath a coat
to secretly retouch a delirious

sunset purchased years ago.
No: I'm talking the weekly

after-hours revisions,
the men toting paint rollers
to touch up fingerprint & scuff

on the bare stretches of wall
between a sleeping gypsy

& Gauguin's Tahiti. I'm talking
the only painters in these galleries
whose one ambition is pure

erasure, whose pinnacle of art
to blend in. Imagine the muscle

of their fluid push & pull,
the effort behind their continuous
mural to anonymity. Let us,

this once, praise Santos & David,
those names no one scrawls,

the brushstrokes no one copies
onto the blank of a sketchpad,
praise, this night, John & Andreas,

their pure heights spattered
with a series of minor frames.

Taste

It's a matter of taste,
they say, whether you prefer
Hopper's lone attendant
serving no one

at the three red gas pumps,
maybe ragging them down

one last time before closing,
or Chagall's woman, heels to sky,
ushering a man toward
two uprooted houses

as though everything was quite
normal, just another day

upside-down in the village.
But a couple of folks
at the museum just might be
greater experts on taste

than any MoMA curator—
two grey-coat security guards,

on one of those long
night shifts when even
that 5th cup of coffee
wasn't enough to save them

from the shadows
of boredom on their rounds,

held a curious contest.
To see who could identify
more artists? More dates of birth
or dates of composition?

No. On this particular night
they had a contest to see

how many paintings
they could lick.
I'm not suggesting
broad, luxurious licks,

just the tip
of the tongue, just

enough to feel stipple
& swirl, the minute ridge
where two strokes overlap.
Who am I going to get in trouble

when I say that the winner
added 57 paintings

to his mouth's tender
catalogue that night?
Disgusting, you might say.
But come on. You know what it's like

to love something so much
you want to come as close

to it as possible, to take it in
as deep as you can, yes,
maybe even to take part
in its becoming or undoing

as if there were a difference.
So go ahead & stick out

your tongue.
Take that fugitive impulse
from the artist's hand
straight into your very gut.

Tell me if the lime-green
of that inverted roof

& the burnt almond
of the filling station's
roadside grasses
live up to their names.

Before You

(For William Matthews, 1942–97)

How like you, Bill, in the end.
Always the first to explore
whatever hip news chanced

our way—the Sanskrit root
of *chutney,* that backup
bassist with all the right

runs. I bet you were always
quick to stake out
a dive, order a drink.

If you were here,
you'd probably hint
what I'm trying to say

is a bit too much like wine
made from pictures of grapes.
But that last season

I took before you a project
I'd started then stalled on
& you said this:

take all your doubts,
draw a circle around them
& give them the finger.

Then you flicked your own finger
from your fist & aimed it
at an imaginary heap

of doubts. So I'm just going
to say it. We miss you.
We miss the sheer velocity

of your presence.
Bill, you beat us out again.
I just thought for once

you'd let someone else
get there before you.

The Ark

You expect the leg-wobble
    & delirium. You expect
        a record winding down.

No easy shot, that backlit
    pacing—the day's tarnished coppers

        so electric they over-brim
the bristled coat—& still
    the park-keeper manages

        a direct hit. But the dart's no
tranquilizer, & so the jaguar's stride

    only escalates to the claws'
        quickened snare.
That's the news footage

    memory plays & replays
        this walk: heightened security,

& this man will thus inoculate
    his whole safari park—kitten
        to camel—against missiles packed

with disease. Midtown,
    all the front pages barking

    invasion, the parks clogged
with dissenters & chanting, & the spare arcs
    of trees doing little to soften

                    the city's stark verticals.
        But then a sight to jar

                even that frenzied jaguar
                        from my mind. Burnt
        orange—a shock of bronze leaves

                decking the trees for a block.
                        A movie crew's grafted to bare trunks

        false branches (indiscriminately
                maples) so for the length
                        of their shoot it's the thick

        of autumn's emblazoning.
                & so on the cusp of war

                        (a *conflict* they'll call it,
        as though it entailed
                spousal insult & not

                        thousands uprooted & scarred,
        & this at best), on the cusp

                of war the street offers up
                        this mock-burgeoning.
        Something consoling

                about standing in their synthetic
                        shade, to know it'll never pass.

        Let's face it: there's no inoculation,
                no immunity for us or those
                        we claim to help,

& the most we can hope for
is the pause these trees afford.

But we know this already,
don't we—that any show of stasis
is always a lie? A week

& they'll all be down,
those leaves ablaze. Down and cleared away

like the hand-lettered signs
of picketers, their leaflets & campaigned
rage. Years from now, the coming weeks

may blanch to a blur. But these two, fused, will always
stay: the riled crowd & their paired-off

rally, this animal panicking
in figure eights, biting at the sting.
How we march these caged streets.

How this stubborn grove
holds us, for a moment,

outside the vanishing.

Fuel

12-ton bus with an eagle
on its side & we all get on
for the plush seats & A/C
because lord it's so fast
it'll get you there
yesterday. This machine's got
a 65-gallon fuel tank
but it doesn't run
on gas. It runs on type A,
type O, type B. It runs on
10,000 hot barrels nuzzled
to 10,000 18-year-old cheeks.
It runs on ghosts. It runs
on 50 newscasters
mouthing from 50 pulsing
screens & they're all talking fuel,
because it runs on cities
taken hostage. It'll knock
on a foreign door at 2 A.M.
& thieve a man from his wife
while she wheels the sky
with her manic arms
because he shares the initials
of a wanted man. It feeds
off sham & deceit
& all who want to be shammed
& deceived. These streets
have always been a billion-eyed
but blind god, & you need
to slap his billion asses
into vision. It runs on the dollar

going up in smoke. It runs
on the lowest orifice
in the highest office. 12-ton bus
with an eagle on its side
& this isn't my stop
but I'm getting off
because I don't know about you
but I can walk from here.

Cure

Up close, it's a million cubes
            of spangle, the robe's saffron
        cleaved, shattered to pixils.

But from beyond the stage
            jeweled with cameras & lilies,

        the dazzled blocks fuse
into the lama's fluid gesticulations
            as he spans the three towered

        screens before the jostling crowd. Shaved
heads & gelled spikes, fingers

            shaped to mudras & frappaccinos,
        & I'm here with Aaron who believes—
this man is the 14th incarnation

            of Chenresig, the embodiment
        of compassion. Arm held

as though to an endless
            string of unanswered questions,
        Aaron raises a recorder to the air,

snaring, he hopes, the occasional
            phrase. *So long as space remains,*

        I'll remain to serve. A rollerblader—
all pivot & gyration—pauses
            to shed his headphones,

mumbles *how about serving me
a large fry and Coke*, then blades off in a blaze

       of spandex. Servitude: we're urged,
    today, to put others before
ourselves—not the lama's

       most honey-coated teaching, but
    who's ever been cured by the taste

of sugar alone?
              Harlem, the week
      of chill & fever no pills
   would soothe, & Aaron insisted

I try *his* doctor ("doctor," he said,
       but the window-front

    was hung with roots, stickered
with rainbows & peace signs,
       neon gnarled to Sanskrit's swag

    & hook—nothing in the least
confidence-inspiring). *Believe,*

       he said. Inside, no introductions.
   No frills of cordiality. Only flasks
& beakers like a mini skyline.

       Aaron & I sat before this frocked
   stranger who began tracing

what appeared to be scripture
        onto a plate, spreading
     not ink but a pulpy tincture of crushed

herbs into prescribed curlicues, deliberate
        dashes. Then, his voice

     turning sudden tumble & surge,
he mouthed the hymn's melismatic
        slur, smeared the sugared

     arabesques into a solution,
& urged me to drink.
              I can't say

        what cured me. But I can urge you—
you on the 'blades—
to take in *these* syllables still crackling

        the speakers before us, this dose
   of extinguished self drawn out

into one fluid intonation
        to glaze your throat:
   the needful pungency,

the honeyed swirls.

Amulet: A Tryptich

i. Ascension

The band's build is anything but tentative—
    cloudburst, startled immersion, & a windowless
        brick room, Englewood cliffs.

For days now I've been trying
    to feel my way into this, Trane's deliberate
        storm. Amorphous squall layered

      & heaped. Bass grind. A shrill
gargle dissolving to background

groans. I'm lost somewhere between
    a seven horn skirmish & cymbal mutiny,
        but such chance commingling sends me back

      to the world—one summer at the school
for the handicapped, the usual classroom

cacophony interrupted by a fit
    of feigned passion: Gary—my charge—
        was imitating porn again, slipping

      his hand down his sweats to a series
of satisfied moans. Eyes shut. Demonic

grin. Then—sudden, rapt gesture—he cocked
    his head to a blank stare. These miniature
        seizures, he sustained a dozen a day—

the four or five seconds of stupor before
the abrupt return, the lights' muted

amber reflooding his retinas. Outside,
    now, wind's tumult gathers to sudden
        lucidity—autumn flaring its first skewed

    contours, the band somehow shaping itself
to an icy blast: rust & copper in hectic

swirls, the leaves' sweep & eddy.
    Then, the ensemble's maelstrom collapses
        to solo, one man bent to push more

    than breath—call it gut, damaged
brawn—past the reed. Result: bandsaw

squeal, wind across a lazy shutter. Fevered
    search to find what the horn can't play
        then play it. And all before he's consumed

    by the group's torrent, his quick scaffold
toppling again to a rush of swirled

cinders, the fierce overflow—cackle, squawk,
    gorgeous rush—to insist that a part of us
        is uncontainable. Because isn't that

    what we *all* want—always to step outside
ourselves? No—perennial exception,

there's Gary, struggling to stay *in*
    his body, though he hardly ever
        knows when he's gone. Is that the reason

for his displays? To more fully occupy
his frame, to claim it as his own

every second he can? Formless clay
        on his desk, & a slab shaped to a slick
                valentine. Brief, determined attention,

        then he's off again. Who knows what's glimpsed
in a seizure—broad, stippled omission?—

but I've watched Gary ascending out of it
        enough times to know this ensemble's
                unyielding persistence (there's not a single

        lapse, no time when the music
isn't) can only be weighed

in silence. Imagine this: abrupt caesura
        bleeding back into the world
                tumultuous & large enough to contain

        this very child, these burnished
horns, the clay heart which could

hold you here, always, now,
        or crumble in your hands.

ii. Swallowtail

The toilet-top aria swelled
          from an appropriately thin & gratified hum
     into a rash slur of vowels

          belted out full-vibrato. I shouldered
the door open & of course
          he was straddling the bowl,

     conducting with grand sweeps
          of his arms, his mouth dilated
around an opera of his own

          making. My first day
     at work in this classroom
          & I knew two things: Gary was eight,

& the crack that cruised
          his mother's veins now heaved
     through his. Back in class,

          a cardboard case with plastic
windows, drab & pendulous
          capsules strung from a branch,

     & we're talking caterpillar, pupa
          & the crowning release. That season
I had my own lessons

          in *Lepidoptera*. I'd always been told
that birds lay off
          because of some bitter

tang. But one courageous
        entomologist sampled their paper-
thin (*flesh*, can you call it?)

        & pronounced them tasteless as dried
toast. The real reason they're left alone
        he discovered far from the milkweed & thistled

    brush, hunched over the bowl. Weeks
        into our class, & the cocoons delayed
& tarried to Gary's ultimate

        impatience—what did these dull sheathes
    have to do with any buoyant
        Sulphur spangling bloom after bloom?

When he grabbed their case
        & shook, eight chrysalises rocked
    on their strings. One tumbled

        to the bottom.
So when we finally
        unsealed the box outside & seven

    lifted over the school walls
        (a staggered drift ever revising
its dwindling contours) one fumbled

        in circles on the ground, tattered
    wings splotched by the pinpricks
        of swollen vessels. Given all the hazards

of pre-birth collisions, you're more than lucky
        if the only body you'll ever have
    can enact all you contain.

Look at you: you were dropped
into your fortunate life, & there's nothing
you can do about it.

How does that go down? Better or worse
than a tasteless butterfly?

iii. Thor's Hammer

Vendors spill out to the curb
        this day of plunged clouds—
    charged vapors
               caught in a fire
escape's delirious tumble—

& the air's alive with *carnations*,
        the word sung, lingering & repeated:
    a woman peddling what's left

in her wicker basket. Crazy
        hibiscus-print skirt all patched
    to mirror her
           tumult
of blooms, & her melody softens the angles

of tables stowed with pewters,
        prismed quartz. Tables tiered
    with the world's burnished

emblems—ankh, cross, scarab,
        & there, in a delicate Celtic
    weave, a tarnish mossed
              silver of Thor's
double-edged hammer. *Good*

fortune, the man says & gives me
        a nod. But even allowing myself
    to thumb its crescent edge,

I can't figure why this piece
                means something to me.
        I can relate
                a share of Norse
tales—the Giants whose hoar-frosted

battalions would topple
                the gods' golden palace in the sky
        if not for Thor, who staved them off

by boomeranging this very tool
                out to the world's rainbowed
        rim. Hurl, catch,
                        repeat,
& the memory returns. Five years back,

the school for the handicapped, & Sarah,
                hunched over her desk, is coloring
        with this token of Thor's hammer on her neck,

her mother's gift a comfort,
                those days when even spoon to mouth's
        a chore. Microcephalic:
                        my first week
in class I learned what this meant:

that Sarah's cranium—usually elastic—
                would never expand, & that one day
        her swelling brain would rupture

on her skull. And so this strange
                prayer: not for the prom or a driver's
        license, but for *stunted*
                        growth, for time
itself to stay. Did anyone ever tell her

the story's conclusion? Would her mind,
          anyway, have fit around the lesson,
     pearled, as it is, to a barb? No staged

bang or thunderclap as a finale,
          only graying Thor's dominions collapsed
     to havoc,
               & the Giants' long shadows
lurching nearer. Constricting

circles. Don't look for poetry here, only
          history: Sarah died last year.
     So I rub the amulet

once & put it down. You can keep
          your good fortune. *Carnations:*
     the woman's song,
                    how sweet
& tremulous it is amid this sun-shot fog.

But what's there to do
          when you can't buy a tool
     or token strong enough for safeguard?

I drop a few coins
          in the woman's basket,
     & start
               walking uptown
with a flower for no one.

A Broken Diptych

i. Imprint

I'm not supposed to
go to the top of these

quarry cliffs. From the top
I can almost see

the river, almost the train
tracks. I have secrets

but I won't tell.
I'm just sifting for clay

ridged with the memory
of shells or the copper

shadows of a fern.
Once an aunt pressed my hand

too heavily into wet slabs
of clay. I didn't know

she was making a fossil
of that hour, so I ran away.

I wouldn't be afraid now.
I look down below all day

until dinner, fingers
against the dust. My handprint

splays on the kitchen wall.
I'm waving at myself.

I'm holding something back.

ii. Glass of Milk

I just missed seeing
a bird fly through

the window like
there was more sky

on this side.
I don't get to see

the games people play
after dark. But

when rasps on the porch
reshuffle into whispers

about a bear,
we all sneak outside

& find my half-
finished glass knocked over

on the deck. The air is cold,
like falling into the creek.

I touch the breath-fogged
rim where his muzzle

had brushed gray moons
of milk. At the edge

of our flashlights, dark pines
still shaking from his heavy

sides. I'm always
just missing out on

secrets. Look: I drank
from the same cup

as that shadow. But now,
in the glass's bottom,

only this mist
of rippling stars.

Seams of Departure

(For Susan Gade Grossman)

i. Cloisters

What was left—after the sieges &
  departures, the best of the rain routed

stonework thieved & dispersed—
   was itself piece by piece dismantled,

the Pyrenean abbey's rubble
   reshuffled into crates & shipped
  to Manhattan's narrowed outskirts,

Fort Tryon Park.
    Sudden bluster
  & squall, the flakes' whirl & eddy—

& so the abbey, reframed here,
   gives a different kind of sanctuary—

no monk's quiet contemplation,
   but us (the hike interrupted,
  the last-second dash) retreating

beneath the rejoined arches . . .

  Healed fractures.
    Three weeks ago,

the trip upstate, & you returned
          after years to face it—your childhood

basement's store of boxes, a more precious
          cargo. You were seven, & years
     have grafted memory to dream: your mother's

life, dim reconstructions.
                    So we looked
          to those parceled remnants—hats,

photos, journals, hand-scrawled
          recipes cradled by an unfinished

Afghan: the tattered seams of departure.
          Then you shrugged—perfect fit—into her
     coat, & the silence of the years

filled our mouths.

                    When I hold you now
     in this 12th-century arcade, dim

palisades of frost edging the Hudson's
          ice-churn below, her jacket's shelter

as much as this ravaged freight
          of column & frieze.
                         Acanthus motif. Scrolling
     leaves. & below, the conjectured base

seamless, almost graceful
          in its steady shouldering.
                         Love, take refuge

here with me, in these stones
      kept standing by what we fill in,

the sever & repair. Let me lend my heat
         to her coat's hemmed embrace
      to hold our fragments together,

keep our fugitive pieces whole.

ii. Kneading

What pale visitations
          tonight, what curious

bedappling—powdered
          fingerprints flowering
counter, sink, light-

          switch, from the sequence
which goes *fold*

          & *push; turn, fold*
& *push*—palm of hand
          flattening, palm spreading

dough as you accompany
          your mother's recipe

to the very smell of childhood,
          the penciled advice to
double the cinnamon,

          & you do. You're alone
in the kitchen, but some nights

          it feels as if there are the two
of you there, brushing
          shoulders over the sweet

bread, the mysteries
          of confection & leavening.

So many things you'd like
        to ask, so much to tell,
but from these few

                mouthfuls—aftertaste
lingering to the crushed

            sugar of cranberry—
it feels at least
                a handful of questions

have been answered
        in the ash & flour,

in this slow blaze
                of the making.

IV

Three Card Monty

First day of spring, a perfect day
        to get hustled. The wide gulf
    of Canal—district of trash & gleam,

people clogging into the street
        for dibs on trinkets or bok choy, litchi,

      wood ears, so many sacks of fortune
cookies it'd take a village
        to contain all the coiled destinies—
    & here, right in the crowd's path,

a man's stacked two cardboard boxes
        into a podium. Looks like the beginning
    of a speech—another stranger's spontaneous

& hectic rant—but instead he quietly
        unpockets three cards & shuffles them

      face down on top. *Find the lady,*
double your money, he wrestles
        his challenge into song, & a fever
    runs over your flesh like a dare

because your blood doesn't know
        what to do with this newfound
    heat & bustle. Guess the queen

of hearts, & you make a quick
        40, & that's how it's going down

now: a man in a suit is winning
repeatedly, pulling in a pile of cash
                for all to see. The bait
        too much, a couple of tourists elbow their way

up front & start dropping 20s. Maybe
                their wills have grafted the queen
        to lady liberty, torch & toga

swapped for a double-faced
                grin. Or maybe they left their loves

        in another country, traded them
for a chance at fortune,
                & now they're in the market
        for a woman, & two dimensional's

better than nothing. In any case,
                they guess wrong again
        & again, & they've put down 100

by the time the man in the suit
                spots the cops & whistles alarm

        so the dealer kicks the boxes
from a podium back to random
                trash, & the two take off together
        around the corner. & the tourists—

their empty wallets are still
                in their hands when they realize
        the suited man was in on the bluff.

But it's only later, over the two beers
            they can muster change for,

        when it occurs to them
that so was that phantom queen
            in her blue & red jewels
            & robes, because by the time

they'd stepped up to win,
            she was slipped up a sleeve,
            nestled to someone else's sweat,

& when it comes down to
            a stranger's luck & life

        she was never even there.

Curses

Gleaned from gutter mouths, we knew their muscle before
meanings, the monosyllables raised to hallowed refrains
on our tongues. We glorified it, the older world of vice
& impiety. So just as we both wanted to be the fugitive
in *cops & robbers*, my best friend & I hid downstairs
& scrawled out a barrage of vulgarities—the heavy hitters,
of course, but then the half-dozen declensions of *ass*,
the lumped phrases of defecation,
the whole shameful lexicon
of anatomy. Then, those white
sheets defiled (microcosm
of our own soiled *tabula rasa*),
we crumpled them &—like shoving a bottled note to
the sea's blind tug—threw them to the ditch at wood's edge.
It was the same fertile gully where I'd picked, years before,
palmfuls of fruit &—the words *monk's hood, nightshade*
still a decade off—swallowed them. I hardly even remember
being sped to the ER to have my stomach pumped. Of course
our ink-spangled pages
never went anywhere,
though I wish I could hold
one now, dim record
of childhood's vast
testing ground—the
necessary absurdity & litter
of it all. Instead, those lost
notes were draped with stray
leaves, coiled with briars
which could never quite
keep from reach those
sweet-looking berries
we were told not to touch,
but had to. And did.

Missing It

Dusk's pitch aftermath.
The skyline's plum is edged
with soot & you're talking

stars. Your Jamaican accent
sends my head back

to the nebula in Orion's belt,

a hazy spill I never see
when I look straight on.

It's your ancestors' blood-spun
craft, you say, to figure
what these vast intersections

auger, & you map out
my birth chart, pointing

to where that murky cluster's

slow wheeling
will lead. Easy to lose track

of a conversation balanced
on such tenuous sounds,
a tumble of phrases

gone forever to night's bleary
corners. But what was ever crucial

that didn't depend

on such unsteady ground?
I lean into your

syllables—my hazy
& shifting future—
catching them all by missing

a bit, listening sideways,
the way we search

for dim bundles of stars.

Signing

The cacophony's blown adrenal
as spring rekindles the streets—

an unmissable pothole aspiring
to a chronic detonation of bass,
castanet of high heels, a hydraulic's

mix of lion roar & lamentation—
but none of these could be

the continuously swinging groove
it looks like this couple is giving
their bodies to: chest-slap

& swivel of wrist, lip pucker,
the two of them absolutely coaxing,

luring each other down the street
to no tune at all. Footfall & shrug,
& he cups his ear

like he didn't hear her
but of course he didn't

because they're only mouthing
the words, & there's a two-beat pause
before it sinks in

this is no modern slam
dance, but language.

What I took for hipster strut
turns gestural slang.
Feel this: with young

love, touch, even the flourish
of a drawn-out breath is a way

of speaking. We have trouble—
you & I—reconstructing the thread
of conversation from the evening

we first met: the double date,
each of us with a partner

we wouldn't choose,
but it was the invitation
of accidental touch,

the way your finger traced the rim
of your glass, that let

attraction go unspoken. Now,
as these two lovers
slip apart, he could be sharing

something as dull as directions,
but I like to think

he was telling her the way
the woozy union of neck
& rhinestone dangle

gives the sky its cerulean
ash & glow, speaking

the way we did—
the sheer physicality
of muscle somehow more pure

than the voice's airy sweep.
Listen: how we let our fingers

speak the moist dialect
of arch & hollow. How
all that our bodies

want to say
will always be

too coarse or refined
for the human tongue.

Shadow & Mirror

One of the East River's half-
         dozen unlikely holdouts (the pier no more
    than whittled pilings, worm-
holed & brackish) & I'm one plank past

              caution, watching Manhattan splinter
         to cobalt flecks, fizzled shards
    of copper—the city, buoyed
              in the current's jeweled slur,

         ascends out of a trembling
    version of itself, its turbulence
              crammed to two dimensions.
    Hard to tell, at first, what sends

    the periodic ringlets shivering
              through the skyline
         until one glimpsed underside—lilac tendrils
    dappled incarnadine—finally reveals

              a flotilla of jelly fish:
         four or five blurred mandalas
    turning (in their myriad modes
              of propulsion) parachute, mushroom, tiger-

         lily, their continuous collapse
    & blossom holding just this side
              of cohesion. What are these creatures
         we unfittingly call "fish"? So little

to see in their liquid frames—shifting
patchwork of river-bottom clay, gravel
& cloud—they *are* what lies behind.
& show me one person in this town

who doesn't in some way smack
of its spangle & rush. We'll allow ourselves
to be taken by the sheer velocity—won't we?—
if there's a chance, somehow,

in this district of shift & flux,
that we can contain an ounce of that shimmer,
that we get to house
a piece of that fixed shining.

Sweet Little Angel

Night-long opus. Fissured
lament. The island
        between Broadway & Sixth,
  & this man cranks out

    song after relentless song—
vigorous calisthenics—till
        his vocal cords just can't
    sustain the workout, & they falter

    to a series of strained growls.
A.M. onrush & we're all quickening
        past while he's ravaged by a chemical
    storm, his body gnarled

    around the blues—*had me*
a sweet little angel, he huffs,
        loved the way she spread her
    wings. Lights shift,

    stranding a crowd of us so close
we *have* to watch—unwilling
        audience held in place
    for the ten seconds of clarity

    we've been allotted each day—
watch as whatever's so tortuously
        embracing him—neither *sweet*
    nor *little*—makes him writhe

against what's left
of a lamp's narrow wash,
            his fingers slicing the beams
        like they were a curtain

he could part to greater light.
& who here among us—waitress
            on her way to a few handfuls
        of change, three corporates noosed

into their ties—who here isn't
driven by some ridiculous
            substance which we feed
        & feed ourselves till it runs

us, till we *become* it? But listen: in this throng
of strangers now suddenly
            paused & fitting their silences
        together, it's hard not to feel

that if you could hush
the subway roll exhaled from pavement,
            hush the city's hoard of alarms & horns
        right down to the last trilling

crickets in the park, if you could
slow your body to a stream
            of warm breath so you're no more
        than the steam easing from the grate

you stand on, you'd hear again,
below the whole mechanical slur
            of Broadway, the faint sweep
        of this man's fingers sliding air.

You'd hear him shaping the angel he'd want
to hold him down,
        to give him back his own body
    in the wake of her kneading hands.

East River View: Renditions

Version: *sun-hammered*
                platinum thrashed to spume,

   the island's transit arterial. Version:
                        splintered to cobalt flecks,
shards of copper . . . Phrases
            gleaned from scratched-out

   attempts, sketches tossed. Nothing
                quite immense enough—shuffle
& reshuffle—to cover the quickening,

   the upheaval festooned & ablaze.
    Try again: *Deep churn*

    of all you don't see: the shattered
cargo of shells, tiny crushed
            spines. The slate of tenement peaks
        gone a sudden coral, & I'm mid-bridge, mid-

   early morning drizzle, catching
    sunrise's story by story disclosure,
                every tenant waking to a different

   rendition of the city. Version:
                turbulent arcs of swept pallor.

Watery palette of shimmer. Let me
            stop. It's task enough to capture
        someone else's attempt,
                    the light twice removed. 1672,

a French engraver's rendering
of this very view: New
Amsterdam's already bustling harbor,

its liquid beltway thronged
with cargo ships & clippers,

the island spied from above.
Not the day's usual inaccuracies—
no clipped vistas, no boundaries roiling
in spatial entropy. Instead: complete

fiction—three concocted hills
bedecked by a city hall, church,
hospital, the requisites checked

off. But further south
the map becomes prophetic:

there, appended to the sprawl,
is a dim preview of today's grid,
blocks spliced by a diagonal.
& so, in this composite

of falsities, the surface pure
fiction, a premonition: Broadway's
erratic forbear. Is this when

your myth began, Protean
city, 1672 & already

you've begun to shape yourself
to someone's *idea* of you,
already you're whatever
we're grasping for? Because now

you're 2,028 blocks & nothing
if not a slim cross-section
of the world's longing. Abrupt

storm: all morning the threat, but in one
moment, the courteous pitter-pat

gives way to the sky's brisk unloading,
& soon, in the water's tribute
to manic commute, there's not a single
gutter that can't find the quickest

route to the river. & it's moments
like these—all a liquid
gush & swell—when only one truth

holds: that any *single* view
will be consumed

& dissolve to the water's drive
& sweep. & if these streets
are ever revising themselves,
tailor-making themselves to each set of eyes,

then the more versions I can furnish,
the closer I come to its great
& palpitating core. So let me fail

in this description again
& again, let me plumb deep

into these roiling
catalogues of water
I'll never get right:
froth-pearled current

subsuming in its pull
                    a plastic earring, a gull
feather, the thirst

        of every parched & burning mouth.

notes

"Mockingbird": 13 miles a day is the speed at which the seasons travel around the globe.

"Strings": The Tibetan Wheel of Life is one of the most common images in Buddhist art, representing many of the realms in which one could be born during the cycles of death and rebirth.

"*The Mustard Seed Garden Manual of Painting*" was a 17th-century Chinese guide.

The scenes in "The Ark" were witnessed during the second Gulf War. A country in the Middle East felt threatened enough by Iraq to inoculate its animals against anthrax. I never discovered the name of the movie set I walked into that day.

"Cure" takes place during the Dalai Lama's visit to Central Park in August 1999.

"Ascension" was recorded by John Coltrane in Rudy Van Gelder's studio in Englewood Cliffs, New Jersey, on June 28, 1965.

"Swallowtail" takes the detail of the curious entomologist from page 258 of Annie Dillard's *Pilgrim at Tinker Creek*.

"A Broken Diptych" is for Zachary, Madison, Ryan, and Brendan.

"Curses" is for Mike B. We actually played a version of Cops & Robbers that we called "Tractor Trailers." Mike knew more bad words than me, I swear.

The view described in "East River View: Renditions" is lifted from Rem Koolhaas's classic, *Delirious New York*, page 15.

Stephen Cramer's first book of poetry, *Shiva's Drum*, was selected for the National Poetry Series by Grace Schulman. His work has appeared in numerous journals, including *Atlanta Review*, *Green Mountains Review*, *New York Quarterly*, and *Southwest Review*. Currently teaching in the Creative Writing program at Johnson State College, he lives with his wife, Joanna, in Burlington, Vermont.

Illinois Poetry Series
Laurence Lieberman, Editor

History Is Your Own Heartbeat
Michael S. Harper (1971)

The Foreclosure
Richard Emil Braun (1972)

The Scrawny Sonnets and Other
Narratives
Robert Bagg (1973)

The Creation Frame
Phyllis Thompson (1973)

To All Appearances: Poems New
and Selected
Josephine Miles (1974)

The Black Hawk Songs
Michael Borich (1975)

Nightmare Begins Responsibility
Michael S. Harper (1975)

The Wichita Poems
Michael Van Walleghen (1975)

Images of Kin: New and
Selected Poems
Michael S. Harper (1977)

Poems of the Two Worlds
Frederick Morgan (1977)

Cumberland Station
Dave Smith (1977)

Tracking
Virginia R. Terris (1977)

Riversongs
Michael Anania (1978)

On Earth as It Is
Dan Masterson (1978)

Coming to Terms
Josephine Miles (1979)

Death Mother and Other Poems
Frederick Morgan (1979)

Goshawk, Antelope
Dave Smith (1979)

Local Men
James Whitehead (1979)

Searching the Drowned Man
Sydney Lea (1980)

With Akhmatova at the
Black Gates
Stephen Berg (1981)

Dream Flights
Dave Smith (1981)

More Trouble with the Obvious
Michael Van Walleghen (1981)

The American Book of the Dead
Jim Barnes (1982)

The Floating Candles
Sydney Lea (1982)

Northbook
Frederick Morgan (1982)

Collected Poems, 1930-83
Josephine Miles (1983; reissue,
1999)

The River Painter
Emily Grosholz (1984)

Healing Song for the Inner Ear
Michael S. Harper (1984)

Good Morning and Good Night
David Wagoner (2005)

American Ghost Roses
Kevin Stein (2005)

Battles and Lullabies
Richard Michelson (2005)

Visiting Picasso
Jim Barnes (2006)

The Disappearing Trick
Len Roberts (2006)

Sleeping with the Moon
Colleen J. McElroy (2007)

Expectation Days
Sandra McPherson (2007)

Tongue & Groove
Stephen Cramer (2007)

The University of Illinois Press
is a founding member of the
Association of American University Presses.

Designed and typeset by
Michael J. Balzano
Manufactured by Thomson-Shore, Inc.

University of Illinois Press
1325 South Oak Street
Champaign, IL 61820-6903
www.press.uillinois.edu